A LOOK AT WORLD

THE BYZANTINE EMPIRE

BY MARY GRIFFIN

Gareth Stevens
PUBLISHING

CRASHCOURSE

Please visit our website, www.garethstevens.com. For a free color catalog of all our high-quality books, call toll free 1-800-542-2595 or fax 1-877-542-2596.

Library of Congress Cataloging-in-Publication Data

Names: Griffin, Mary, 1978- author.
Title: The Byzantine Empire / Mary Griffin.
Description: New York : Gareth Stevens Publishing, 2020. | Series: A look at
  world history | Includes index.
Identifiers: LCCN 2018039205| ISBN 9781538241301 (pbk.) | ISBN 9781538241325
  (library bound) | ISBN 9781538241318 (6 pack)
Subjects: LCSH: Byzantine Empire--Civilization--Juvenile literature.
Classification: LCC DF521 .G75 2020 | DDC 949.5/02--dc23
LC record available at https://lccn.loc.gov/2018039205

First Edition

Published in 2020 by
Gareth Stevens Publishing
111 East 14th Street, Suite 349
New York, NY 10003

Copyright © 2020 Gareth Stevens Publishing

Designer: Katelyn E. Reynolds
Editor: Therese Shea

Photo credits: Cover, p. 1 Fine Art Images/Heritage Images/Getty Images; cover,
pp. 1–32 (background) javarman/Shutterstock.com; cover, pp. 1–32 (border)
Anastasiia Smiian/Shutterstock.com; p. 5 Universal History Archive/Getty Images;
p. 7 Di Gregorio Giulio/Shutterstock.com; p. 9 (map) dikobraziy/Shutterstock.com;
p. 9 (inset) Cesarz/Shutterstock.com; p. 11 Richard T. Nowitz/Corbis Documentary/
Getty Images; p. 13 ZU_09/DigitalVision Vectors/Getty Images; p. 15 The Yorck Project
(2002) 10.000 Meisterwerke der Malerei (DVD-ROM), distributed by DIRECTMEDIA
Publishing GmbH. ISBN: 3936122202./TRAJAN 117/Wikipedia.org; p. 17 De Agostini/
G. Dagli Orti/Getty Images; p. 19 Hello world/Wikipedia.org; p. 21 Dianelos Georgoudis/
Soerfm/Wikipedia.org; p. 23 Prisma/UIG/Getty Images; p. 25 Mehmet Cetin/Shutterstock.com;
p. 27 Fototeca Gilardi/Getty Images; p. 29 Benjamin Constant/Getty Images.

Printed in the United States of America

CPSIA compliance information: Batch #CS19GS: For further information contact Gareth Stevens, New York, New York at 1-800-542-2595.

CONTENTS

Words in the glossary appear in **bold** type the first time they are used in the text.

AN EMPIRE WITHIN AN EMPIRE

The Byzantine **Empire** began as the eastern part of the Roman Empire. However, it lasted nearly 1,000 years after the western part of the Roman Empire fell. Some parts of Byzantine **culture** have lasted even into the present day.

ROMAN EMPIRE,
A.D. 117.

MAKE THE GRADE

The eastern part of the Roman Empire wasn't
called the Byzantine Empire
until the 1600s, after it had ended.

5

At its largest, the Roman Empire controlled a huge amount of territory, including much of Europe, parts of eastern Asia, and northern Africa. Rome was its capital and where its rulers, or emperors, lived. However, ruling such a large empire was hard.

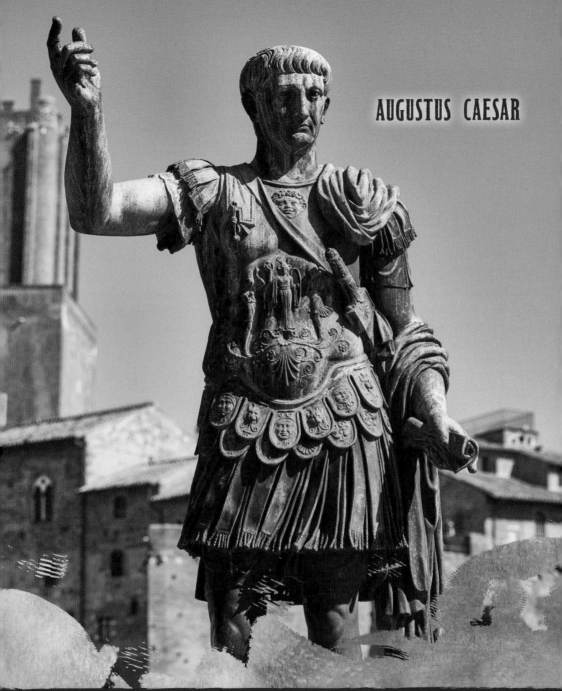

AUGUSTUS CAESAR

MAKE THE GRADE

The Roman Republic was founded in 509 BC.
It became the Roman Empire when Augustus
Caesar was named its first emperor in 27 BC.

7

Emperor Diocletian ruled
the Roman Empire from
AD 284 to 305. He
separated it in two so it
could be controlled better.
The west was ruled from
Rome, and the east
was ruled from the city
of Byzantium.

DIOCLETIAN

DIOCLETIANVS

BLACK SEA

BYZANTIUM

BOSPORUS

SEA OF
MARMARA

AEGEAN
SEA

MEDITERRANEAN SEA

MAKE THE GRADE

Byzantium was located in Europe near
the Bosporus, a narrow body of water that
connects the Black Sea to the Sea of Marmara.
The Byzantine Empire was named for Byzantium.

THE NEW ROME

The Roman Empire was made whole again by Constantine I, who ruled over all of it. In AD 330, Constantine chose Byzantium to be the "new Rome," or the new capital of the Roman Empire. He called the city "Constantinople," after himself.

CONSTANTINE I

MAKE THE GRADE

Constantinople was located between
Roman territory in both Europe
and the western part of Asia.

11

The Roman Empire was divided again under Theodosius I, who ruled from AD 379 to 395. The emperor of the western part of the Roman Empire, Romulus Augustus, was overthrown in AD 476. However, the eastern part of the empire continued to grow.

MAKE THE GRADE

Romulus Augustus was removed from power
by a **Germanic** king. This is considered
to be the end of the Roman Empire.

13

JUSTINIAN I

The Byzantine Empire's borders changed throughout its existence. It was at its largest during the time of Emperor Justinian I, who ruled from AD 527 to 565. It stretched from Spain in the west to the Middle East and from southern Europe to northern Africa.

JUSTINIAN I

MAKE THE GRADE

The Justinian Code was a collection
of Roman laws. The code influenced
later laws in many countries.

15

THE GOLDEN AGE

From about AD 641 to 1025, the Byzantine Empire was in its **golden age**. Its military was mighty, and its **religion** and art spread throughout its territory and beyond. Byzantine money became the most important **currency** in Europe.

COIN SHOWING BASIL I
AND HIS SON CONSTANTINE

MAKE THE GRADE

Beginning in 867 with Basil I,
the Byzantine Empire was ruled by
Macedonian emperors, who came from
an area northeast of today's Greece.

17

RELIGION

In AD 313, Constantine I made Christianity a legal religion in the Roman Empire. It later became the official religion. Differences in religious practices in the west and east created a **schism** (SIH-zehm) in the church in 1054. Eastern Orthodox Christianity became the religion of the Eastern Roman Empire.

CONSTANTINE I

ΠΙΣΤΥΟΜΕΝ ΕΙΣ ΕΝΑ ΘΝ, ΠΑΤΕΡΑ ΠΑΝΤΟΚΡΑΤΡΑ, ΠΟΙΗΤΗΝ ΟΥΡΑΝΟΥ Κ ΓΗΣ
ΟΡΑΤΩΝ ΤΕ ΠΑΝΤΩΝ Κ ΑΟΡΑΤΩΝ. ΚΕΙΣ ΕΝΑ ΚΝ ΙΗΣΥΝ ΧΝ ΤΝ ΥΙΟΝ
ΤΥ ΘΥ ΤΝ ΜΝΟΓΕΝΗ, ΤΝ ΕΚ ΤΥ ΠΡΟΣ ΓΕΝΝΗΘΕΝΤΑ ΠΡΟ ΠΑΝΤΩΝ ΤΝ ΑΙΩΝΩ
ΦΩΣ ΕΚ ΦΩΤΟΣ ΘΕΟΝ ΑΛΗΘΙΝΟΝ ΕΚ ΘΕΥ ΑΛΗΘΙΝΥ ΓΕΝΝΘΕΝΤΑ ΟΥ
ΠΟΙΗΘΕΝΤΑ, ΟΜΟΥΣΙΟΝ ΤΩ ΠΡΙ ΔΙ Υ ΤΑ ΠΑΝΤΑ ΕΓΕΝΕΤΟ ΤΟ ΔΙ ΗΜΑΣ ΤΟΥΣ
ΑΝΘΡΩΠΥΣ Κ ΔΑ ΤΗΝ ΗΜΕΤΕΡΑΝ ΣΩΤΗΡΙΑΝ ΚΑΤΕΛΘΟΝΤΑ ΕΚ ΤΩ ΟΥΡΑΝΩ
Κ ΣΑΡΚΩΘΕΝΤΑ ΕΚ ΠΝΥΜΑΤΟΣ ΑΓΙΥ Κ ΜΑΡΙΑΣ ΤΗΣ ΠΑΡΘΕΝΥ ΚΕΝΑΝΘΡΩ
ΠΗΣΑΝΤΑ. ΣΑΥΡΩΘΕΝΤΑ ΤΕ ΥΠΕΡ ΗΜΩ ΕΠΙ ΠΟΝΤΙΥ ΠΙΛΑΤΥ
ΚΑΙ ΠΑΘΟΝΤΑ, Κ ΤΑΦΕΝΤΑ...

MAKE THE GRADE

Eastern Orthodox Christianity
later became the major religion
in Russia as well as Greece.

19

ART AND ARCHITECTURE

Byzantine art was largely focused on religion. It included mosaics, which are pictures made of colorful pieces of stone or glass. Mosaics covered walls and ceilings of churches. Byzantine artistic style changed little over the hundreds of years the empire lasted.

MAKE THE GRADE

Most Byzantine artwork was anonymous, which means the artist didn't sign it or tell others they had done it.

21

Another important form of Byzantine art was manuscript illumination. Illuminated manuscripts were handmade books, often about Christianity. They had illustrations, or pictures, along with words. Some artists used gold and silver to color them. Illuminated manuscripts helped spread the Byzantine art style.

MAKE THE GRADE

More than 40,000 Byzantine
illuminated manuscripts
have survived to present day.

Byzantine **architecture** is known for its large domes. The Hagia (HAY-jee-uh) Sophia was built as a Christian church in the 6th century in Constantinople. It was the largest church in the world for hundreds of years.

MAKE THE GRADE

In the 1400s, the Hagia Sophia
was made into a mosque, which is
a building for Muslim religious services.

THE END OF THE EMPIRE

In the late 11th century, a "holy war" began between Christians and Muslims. Byzantine emperor Alexius I asked countries in the west for help against Muslims **threatening** the city of Constantinople. They agreed, and the First Crusade began.

MAKE THE GRADE

During the Fourth Crusade (1202–1204),
Christian soldiers from western Europe
took Constantinople for themselves,
though it was recaptured in 1261.

27

The Crusades greatly weakened the Byzantine Empire. On May 29, 1453, the Ottoman Turks, from the area that's now Turkey, **conquered** Constantinople. Emperor Constantine XI Palaeologus was killed in the fighting. The Byzantine Empire came to an end.

MAKE THE GRADE

Constantinople was made the capital
of the Ottoman Empire. It later
became known as Istanbul.

29

KEY DATES OF THE BYZANTINE EMPIRE

509 BC
The Roman Republic is founded.

27 BC
Augustus Caesar becomes ruler of the Roman Empire.

AD 285
Emperor Diocletian separates the Roman Empire into halves.

330
Emperor Constantine I chooses Byzantium, or Constantinople, to be the capital of the Roman Empire.

476
Emperor Romulus Augustus is overthrown. The Western Roman Empire ends.

527
Emperor Justinian I begins his rule. The Byzantine Empire grows to be its largest.

537
The Hagia Sophia is completed.

867
Basil I becomes the first of the Macedonian emperors.

1054
A schism occurs in the Catholic Church. Eastern Orthodox Christianity became the religion of the Byzantine Empire.

1096
The First Crusade begins.

1453
Ottoman Turks conquer Constantinople. The Byzantine Empire ends.

GLOSSARY

architecture: a style of building

conquer: to take by force

culture: the beliefs and ways of life of a group of people

currency: the money a country uses

empire: a large area of land under the control of a single ruler

Germanic: a term used by ancient Romans for peoples living in northern central Europe

golden age: a time of great happiness, success, and achievement

influence: to have an effect on

Muslim: a follower of the religion of Islam

religion: a belief in and way of honoring a god or gods

republic: a form of government in which the people elect representatives who run the government

schism: a split among the members of a group that occurs because they disagree on something

threaten: to say or act like you will harm someone or something

FOR MORE INFORMATION

BOOKS

Kovacs, Vic. *The Culture of the Byzantine Empire*. New York, NY: PowerKids Press, 2017.

VanVoorst, Jenny Fretland. *The Byzantine Empire*. North Mankato, MN: Compass Point Books, 2013.

WEBSITES

Byzantine Empire
www.history.com/topics/ancient-history/byzantine-empire
Read more about the history of this interesting empire.

Middle Ages: Byzantine Empire
www.ducksters.com/history/middle_ages_byzantine_empire.php
Find important facts about the Byzantine Empire here.

INDEX